Getting from Here to There

by Antonia Barber

NATIONAL GEOGRAPHIC LEARNING | CENGAGE

How do people get to work? How do they get to school? How do they get to their favorite places?

In Tokyo, Japan, many people take the subway. The subway runs under the city.

These men push people onto a crowded subway.

People also take fast trains
between cities.

This train can go
186 miles per hour.

 Many people in Mexico City take the train.

They ride in buses, too.

Some buses in Mexico City are for women and children only.

 In Mumbai, India, many people take the bus. Many buses have two levels.

People sometimes ride in yellow and
black taxis like this one . . .

or in taxis like this one.

This taxi
is called
an *auto
rickshaw*.

People ride in taxis in Havana, Cuba, too. They ride in taxis that look like this . . .

or this . . .

or this!

This taxi is called a *coco taxi* because it looks like a coconut.

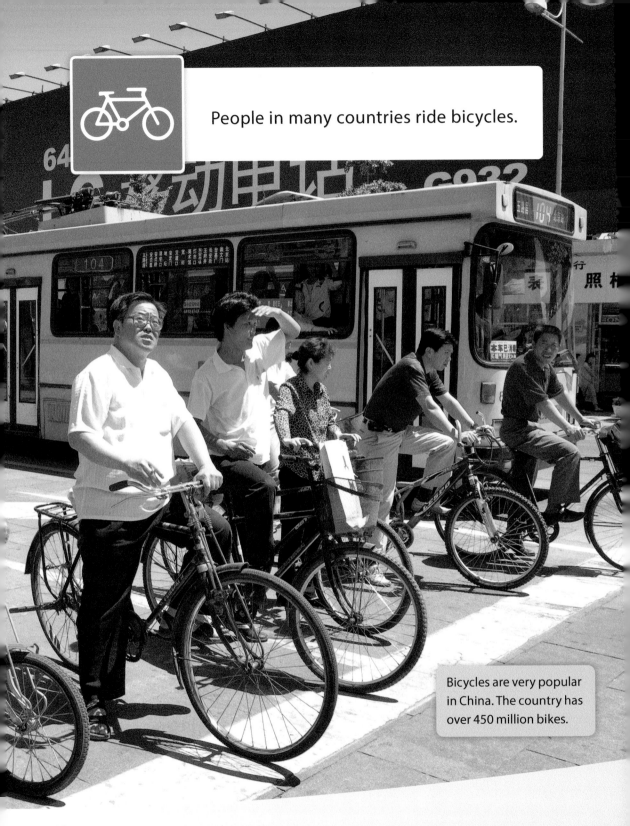

People in many countries ride bicycles.

Bicycles are very popular in China. The country has over 450 million bikes.

Bicycles are cheap, and they don't pollute the air.

Many countries have bike paths, like this one in the Netherlands.

People carry things on their bikes. This boy in Uganda carries bananas.

 Some people take a ferry to their jobs.

The Staten Island Ferry takes people back and forth across New York Harbor.

People and cars can go on this ferry in Egypt.

There are many different ways to get from here to there. But sometimes the best way to go is on your own two feet!